Morgan Ridge

STAR WARS EPISODE 1: JEDI POWER BATTLES GAME GUIDE

Step-by-Step Walkthroughs, Hidden Power-Ups, and Masterful Combat Techniques

© 2025 Morgan Ridge. All rights reserved.
This guide, including all written content, graphics, and designs, is protected under copyright law. Unauthorized reproduction, distribution, or use of any part of this publication is strictly prohibited without prior written permission from the author.

CHAPTER 1: INTRODUCTION TO JEDI POWER BATTLES ___ *6*

1.1 INSTALLATION PROCESS _____ 6

1.2 BACKGROUND AND DEVELOPMENT _____ 9

1.3 OVERVIEW OF GAMEPLAY MECHANICS _____ 10

1.4 KEY FEATURES AND APPEAL _____ 12

1.5 TARGET AUDIENCE AND PURPOSE OF THE GUIDE _____ 14

1.5 TARGET AUDIENCE AND PURPOSE OF THE GUIDE _____ 15

CHAPTER 2: JEDI HEROES AND UNLOCKABLE CHARACTERS _____ *17*

2.2 MACE WINDU AND PLO KOON _____ 19

2.3 UNLOCKABLE CHARACTERS: QUEEN AMIDALA, CAPTAIN PANAKA, AND DARTH MAUL _____ 21

2.4 CHARACTER STRENGTHS AND COMBAT STYLES _____ 24

CHAPTER 3: COMBAT SYSTEM AND FORCE ABILITIES ____ *25*

3.1 LIGHTSABER COMBAT TECHNIQUES _____ 25

3.2 FORCE POWERS: USAGE AND STRATEGIES _____ 27

3.3 COMBOS AND SPECIAL MOVES _____ 29

3.4 DEFENSIVE TACTICS AND DODGING _____ 30

CHAPTER 4: LEVEL 1 - TRADE FEDERATION BATTLESHIP _*32*

4.1 WALKTHROUGH: CORRIDOR NAVIGATION AND DROID COMBAT _____ 32

4.2 BOSS STRATEGY: LOADER DROID _____ 34

4.3 HIDDEN POWER-UPS AND POINTS GUIDE _____ 36

4.4 AVOIDING CONVEYOR BELT HAZARDS _____ 37

CHAPTER 5: LEVEL 2 - SWAMPS OF NABOO _____ *40*

- 5.1 NAVIGATING THE SWAMP AND TREE CLIMB _____ 40
- 5.2 STAMPEDE AVOIDANCE TACTICS _____ 42
- 5.3 GUNGAN ARTIFACT LOCATION _____ 43
- 5.4 BOSS STRATEGY: GIANT WORM _____ 45

CHAPTER 6: LEVEL 3 - CITY OF THEED _____ 48
- 6.1 HANDMAIDEN RESCUE LOCATIONS _____ 48
- 6.2 LOW ROAD VS. HIGH ROAD: WHICH PATH TO TAKE ____ 50
- 6.3 USING THE AAT TANK EFFECTIVELY _____ 52
- 6.4 BOSS STRATEGY: DROIDEKA DEFENSE DROID _____ 54

CHAPTER 7: LEVEL 5 - TATOOINE _____ 58
- 7.1 PROTECTING ANAKIN AND RETRIEVING THE HYPERDRIVE _____ 58
- 7.2 SURVIVING SANDSTORMS AND PROBE DROIDS _____ 60
- 7.3 GUNGAN ARTIFACT COLLECTION _____ 61
- 7.4 BOSS STRATEGY: DARTH MAUL _____ 63

CHAPTER 8: BONUS LEVELS AND CHALLENGES _____ 66
- 8.1 LEVEL 11: DROIDEKAS _____ 66
- 8.2 LEVEL 12: KAADU RACE _____ 68
- 8.3 LEVEL 13: GUNGAN ROUNDUP _____ 69
- 8.4 LEVEL 14: SURVIVAL CHALLENGE _____ 71

CHAPTER 9: ADVANCED TIPS AND SECRETS _____ 74
- 9.1 MAXIMIZING POINTS AND BONUSES _____ 74
- 9.2 UNLOCKING CONCEPT ART AND EXTRAS _____ 76
- 9.3 EXPLORING HIDDEN ROUTES AND POWER-UPS _____ 78

9.4 CO-OP MULTIPLAYER STRATEGIES _____ 80

CHAPTER 10: FINAL BOSS AND ENDGAME STRATEGIES___83

    10.1 LEVEL 10 WALKTHROUGH: THE FINAL BATTLE _____ 83

    10.2 BOSS STRATEGY: DEFEATING DARTH MAUL _____ 84

    10.3 ENERGY BRIDGE AND CATWALK NAVIGATION_____ 87

    10.4 LASER MAZE AND ULTIMATE VICTORY_____ 88

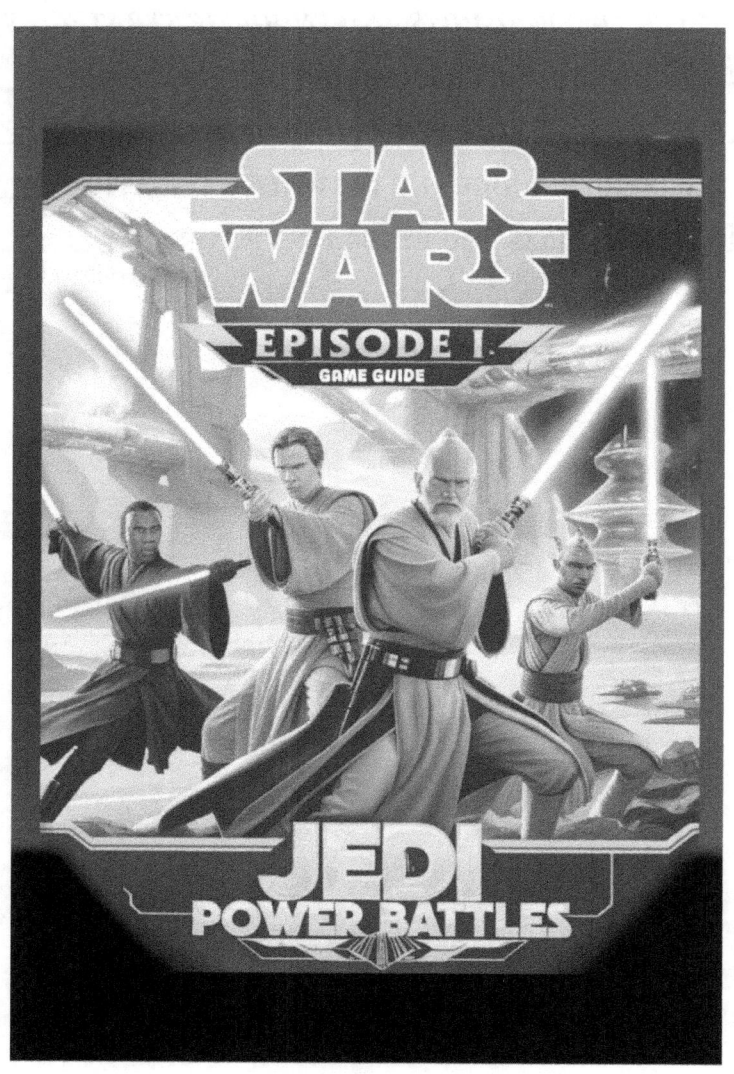

CHAPTER 1: INTRODUCTION TO JEDI POWER BATTLES

1.1 INSTALLATION PROCESS

Installing *Star Wars: Episode I: Jedi Power Battles* is a straightforward process, but ensuring the game runs smoothly requires attention to a few key steps. This guide will walk you through the installation process for various platforms where the game is available.

For PlayStation (Original Console Version)

1. **Insert the Disc**: Begin by placing the game disc into your PlayStation console. Ensure the console is powered on and the disc is clean to avoid any read errors.
2. **Start the Game**: Once the console recognizes the disc, navigate to the "Start Game" option on the home screen.
3. **Memory Card Check**: Ensure you have sufficient space on your memory card to save your progress. *Jedi Power Battles* requires a minimum of one memory block.

4. **Adjust Settings**: Use the options menu to configure controls, screen brightness, and sound preferences to your liking before diving into the game.

For PlayStation 2 (Backward Compatibility)

1. **Insert the Disc**: Place the original PlayStation disc into the PlayStation 2 console. Ensure the console is set to backward compatibility mode.
2. **Access Settings**: Go to the options menu to enhance graphics and load times, as the PlayStation 2 offers slight improvements for original PlayStation games.
3. **Save Game Setup**: Use a PlayStation 1 memory card for saving progress, as PlayStation 2 memory cards are incompatible with original PlayStation games.

For Emulators (PC Version)

1. **Obtain the Game ROM**: Legally acquire a copy of the game ROM. Ensure it's from a reputable source to avoid corrupted files.
2. **Install an Emulator**: Download a trusted PlayStation emulator such as ePSXe or RetroArch. Follow the emulator's setup instructions to configure controls and graphics.

3. **Load the ROM**: Open the emulator and load the *Jedi Power Battles* ROM file. Adjust settings for optimal performance, such as resolution and frame rate.
4. **Save States**: Take advantage of emulator save states to create additional backup points during gameplay.

For Modern Consoles (Digital Re-releases)

If the game is re-released digitally on modern platforms like PlayStation Network, the installation process becomes even easier:

1. **Purchase and Download**: Buy the game from the digital store and download it to your console.
2. **Automatic Installation**: Once downloaded, the game will install automatically.
3. **Updates and Patches**: Check for any updates or patches to ensure the game runs smoothly.
4. **Cloud Saves**: Utilize cloud saving options for seamless progress backups.

Troubleshooting Common Issues

- **Disc Read Errors**: Clean the disc gently with a microfiber cloth, moving from the center outward. Avoid using abrasive materials.
- **Emulator Performance Problems**: Update the emulator software and ensure your PC meets the required specifications for smooth gameplay.
- **Save File Corruption**: Always use legitimate hardware or software to avoid corrupted save files.

1.2 BACKGROUND AND DEVELOPMENT

The creation of *Star Wars: Episode I: Jedi Power Battles* was born out of a desire to bring the dynamic action of *The Phantom Menace* to gamers. Developed by LucasArts, the game was a testament to their dedication to crafting authentic *Star Wars* experiences. As one of the leading developers of *Star Wars* titles, LucasArts had the challenge of creating a game that would complement the cinematic release while standing on its own as an engaging, replayable experience.

The team drew heavily from the film's lore, capturing the essence of the Jedi Order's battle against the rising forces of the Sith. From the intricate corridors of the Trade Federation

Battleship to the serene but perilous swamps of Naboo, the game's environments were meticulously designed to mirror the movie's aesthetic. The development process also involved close collaboration with Lucasfilm to ensure that the game adhered to the overarching *Star Wars* canon.

The game was released for the PlayStation, Dreamcast, and Game Boy Advance, each platform offering slightly different gameplay experiences. The PlayStation version, with its cooperative mode and intricate level design, quickly became a fan favorite. Despite some criticism for its challenging difficulty and occasionally frustrating camera angles, the game's engaging combat and deep connection to the *Star Wars* universe solidified its place as a beloved entry in the franchise.

1.3 OVERVIEW OF GAMEPLAY MECHANICS

At its core, *Jedi Power Battles* is an action-adventure game that demands strategic combat, precise platforming, and quick reflexes. The game's mechanics are straightforward yet layered, offering depth for those willing to master its intricacies.

Combat

Combat is the centerpiece of the gameplay, and each Jedi brings unique abilities to the table. Lightsaber combat is fluid and satisfying, allowing players to string together combos for maximum damage. Players can also deflect blaster bolts, adding a layer of strategy as they time their moves to avoid taking damage. Force powers further enhance combat, enabling players to push enemies, perform powerful area attacks, or heal themselves in critical moments.

Platforming

Platforming sections are interspersed throughout the game, requiring players to navigate treacherous terrain. These sections test timing and precision, as missing a jump can often result in falling to one's doom. While challenging, the platforming adds variety to the gameplay, ensuring that players remain engaged.

Multiplayer Mode

One of the standout features is the cooperative multiplayer mode. This mode allows two players to tackle the game's levels together, sharing power-ups and strategizing to overcome difficult sections. The cooperative mode not only enhances replayability but also brings an added layer of fun as players work together to defeat enemies and navigate the galaxy.

Scoring System

The game's scoring system encourages players to perform well in combat, collect power-ups, and explore levels thoroughly. Bonuses are awarded for achieving high scores, adding an element of competition and motivation to revisit levels.

1.4 KEY FEATURES AND APPEAL

Diverse Characters

The game's roster includes five playable Jedi, each with distinct abilities and playstyles. Obi-Wan Kenobi and Qui-Gon Jinn offer balanced combat capabilities, while Mace Windu's powerful attacks make him a formidable force. Plo Koon's agility and Adi Gallia's mastery of Force powers add depth and variety.

Unlockable characters like Queen Amidala and Darth Maul provide additional incentives for players to replay the game.

Immersive Levels

The levels in *Jedi Power Battles* are designed with care, blending action, exploration, and platforming. From the bustling streets of Theed to the deserts of Tatooine, each level feels unique and richly detailed. Hidden power-ups and alternate paths encourage players to explore every corner of the map.

Challenging Boss Fights

Boss battles are a highlight of the game, offering intense encounters that test players' combat skills and strategy. From facing off against the towering Loader Droid to the climactic duel with Darth Maul, these battles are both challenging and rewarding.

Nostalgia Factor

For fans of *The Phantom Menace*, the game serves as a nostalgic journey through some of the movie's most iconic moments. The inclusion of John Williams' score and authentic sound effects further immerses players in the *Star Wars* universe.

1.5 TARGET AUDIENCE AND PURPOSE OF THE GUIDE

Diverse Characters

The game's roster includes five playable Jedi, each with distinct abilities and playstyles. Obi-Wan Kenobi and Qui-Gon Jinn offer balanced combat capabilities, while Mace Windu's powerful attacks make him a formidable force. Plo Koon's agility and Adi Gallia's mastery of Force powers add depth and variety. Unlockable characters like Queen Amidala and Darth Maul provide additional incentives for players to replay the game.

Immersive Levels

The levels in *Jedi Power Battles* are designed with care, blending action, exploration, and platforming. From the bustling streets of Theed to the deserts of Tatooine, each level feels unique and richly detailed. Hidden power-ups and alternate paths encourage players to explore every corner of the map.

Challenging Boss Fights

Boss battles are a highlight of the game, offering intense encounters that test players' combat skills and strategy. From facing off against the towering Loader Droid to the climactic duel with Darth Maul, these battles are both challenging and rewarding.

Nostalgia Factor

For fans of *The Phantom Menace*, the game serves as a nostalgic journey through some of the movie's most iconic moments. The inclusion of John Williams' score and authentic sound effects further immerses players in the *Star Wars* universe.

1.5 TARGET AUDIENCE AND PURPOSE OF THE GUIDE

Target Audience

This guide is designed for a broad audience:

- **New Players**: Detailed explanations of mechanics and strategies ensure that newcomers can easily pick up the game and enjoy its challenges.

- **Experienced Gamers**: Advanced tips and hidden secrets cater to seasoned players looking to master the game and achieve high scores.
- **Star Wars Enthusiasts**: Fans of the franchise will appreciate the detailed lore connections and character insights provided throughout the guide.

Purpose

The purpose of this guide is to provide a comprehensive resource for players at all skill levels. Whether you're struggling to navigate the platforming sections or looking for strategies to defeat Darth Maul, this guide offers clear, actionable advice. In addition, it celebrates the rich universe of *Star Wars*, delving into the lore and design choices that make the game a timeless classic.

By combining in-depth walkthroughs, character analyses, and advanced gameplay strategies, this guide aims to be an indispensable companion for anyone venturing into the galaxy of *Jedi Power Battles*.

CHAPTER 2: JEDI HEROES AND UNLOCKABLE CHARACTERS

As two of the most iconic Jedi from *The Phantom Menace*, Obi-Wan Kenobi and Qui-Gon Jinn are a perfect starting point for players exploring *Jedi Power Battles*. Each character's abilities and fighting style reflect their personalities and roles within the Star Wars universe.

Obi-Wan Kenobi

Obi-Wan Kenobi is an excellent choice for players seeking a balanced approach to combat. His proficiency with the lightsaber and adaptability make him ideal for beginners and veterans alike. Obi-Wan's attacks combine speed and precision, allowing players to chain combos effectively.

Strengths

- **Balanced Combat**: Excels in both offensive and defensive gameplay.

- **Combo Mastery**: Easy-to-learn combos that are effective against various enemy types.
- **Force Abilities**: His Force Push is perfect for crowd control.

Weaknesses

- **Average Power**: Lacks the brute strength of other characters like Mace Windu.
- **Limited Range**: Relies heavily on close combat.

Qui-Gon Jinn

Qui-Gon Jinn embodies wisdom and resilience, bringing a calm yet powerful presence to the battlefield. His attacks are deliberate, focusing on delivering heavy damage with well-placed strikes.

Strengths

- **High Damage Output**: Deals significant damage with fewer hits.
- **Force Abilities**: His Force Heal is invaluable for sustaining health.
- **Defensive Mastery**: Excellent at deflecting blaster bolts and countering enemies.

Weaknesses

- **Slower Attacks**: Requires precise timing for effective combos.
- **Mobility**: Slightly less agile compared to other characters.

Together, Obi-Wan and Qui-Gon provide a balanced duo, allowing players to choose between speed and power depending on their playstyle. Their synergy in co-op mode makes them a formidable team.

2.2 MACE WINDU AND PLO KOON

Mace Windu and Plo Koon bring unique attributes to the game, each offering a distinct gameplay experience that caters to different player preferences.

Mace Windu

Known for his combat prowess and commanding presence, Mace Windu is the powerhouse of the Jedi roster. His aggressive fighting style and raw strength make him a favorite for players who enjoy dominating enemies in close combat.

Strengths

- **High Strength**: Delivers devastating blows to enemies.
- **Wide Attack Range**: His lightsaber swings cover a large area, making him effective against groups.
- **Resilience**: Can take more damage than other characters.

Weaknesses

- **Slow Combos**: Requires patience and precision to execute attacks.
- **Force Abilities**: Limited versatility compared to other Jedi.

Plo Koon

Plo Koon is a master of agility and speed, offering a playstyle that emphasizes movement and quick strikes. His finesse on the battlefield makes him an excellent choice for players who value precision.

Strengths

- **Agility**: Moves quickly and dodges attacks with ease.
- **Force Abilities**: His Force Lightning is unique and highly effective.

- **Combo Potential**: Can chain attacks seamlessly for maximum damage.

Weaknesses

- **Lower Defense**: Requires careful positioning to avoid damage.
- **Short Range**: Relies on closing the distance to enemies quickly.

Mace Windu and Plo Koon represent opposite ends of the combat spectrum one relying on brute force and the other on finesse. Players can experiment with both to find their preferred style.

2.3 UNLOCKABLE CHARACTERS: QUEEN AMIDALA, CAPTAIN PANAKA, AND DARTH MAUL

Unlockable characters add depth and replayability to *Jedi Power Battles*, each bringing their own unique abilities and quirks.

Queen Amidala

As a non-Jedi character, Queen Amidala relies on agility and ranged attacks. Her inclusion adds a fresh perspective, emphasizing strategy over raw power.

Strengths

- **Ranged Combat**: Equipped with a blaster for long-range attacks.
- **Agility**: Quick movements allow her to evade enemies easily.

Weaknesses

- **Limited Damage**: Blaster attacks are weaker than lightsabers.
- **No Force Abilities**: Relies solely on physical attacks and positioning.

Captain Panaka

Captain Panaka offers a balanced approach, combining ranged combat with solid defense. His ability to block blaster bolts makes him a versatile choice.

Strengths

- **Versatility**: Effective in both offense and defense.

- **Team Support**: Can provide cover for other players in co-op mode.

Weaknesses

- **Average Mobility**: Slower than other characters.
- **Limited Combos**: Lacks advanced attack chains.

Darth Maul

Darth Maul is the ultimate unlockable character, bringing the dark side's ferocity to the game. His double-bladed lightsaber and devastating Force abilities make him a powerhouse.

Strengths

- **High Damage Output**: Excels in dealing massive damage.
- **Force Abilities**: Includes Force Choke and Force Lightning.
- **Intimidating Presence**: Strikes fear into enemies.

Weaknesses

- **Energy Reliant**: Drains Force energy quickly.
- **Challenging to Master**: Requires skill to utilize effectively.

2.4 CHARACTER STRENGTHS AND COMBAT STYLES

Each character in *Jedi Power Battles* brings unique strengths and combat styles, allowing players to tailor their experience. Whether you prefer raw power, agility, or strategic finesse, there's a character suited to your playstyle. Experimentation is key to mastering the game, and understanding each character's strengths and weaknesses will give you an edge in the galaxy's toughest battles.

CHAPTER 3: COMBAT SYSTEM AND FORCE ABILITIES

3.1 LIGHTSABER COMBAT TECHNIQUES

The lightsaber is the signature weapon of the Jedi and Sith, embodying both elegance and power. In *Star Wars: Episode I: Jedi Power Battles*, mastering lightsaber combat is essential for overcoming enemies and progressing through the game's challenging levels. Each Jedi has a distinct combat style that enhances the gameplay experience, and understanding these nuances will elevate your skills.

Basic Attacks

Each Jedi begins with a repertoire of basic attacks, including quick slashes and heavy strikes. Quick slashes are ideal for dispatching weaker enemies, while heavy strikes deal significant damage but require more time to execute. Learning when to use each is key to efficient combat.

Advanced Lightsaber Techniques

1. **Directional Attacks**: Combining movement with attack buttons allows for directional strikes, enabling players to target enemies from different angles. This is particularly useful for crowd control.
2. **Aerial Strikes**: By jumping and attacking mid-air, players can execute devastating aerial strikes. These are particularly effective against taller enemies or those positioned on higher platforms.
3. **Parries and Ripostes**: Timing is everything in a duel. Parrying an enemy's attack opens them up to a counterstrike, providing a tactical advantage.

Environmental Interactions

Lightsabers aren't just for combat. Players can use them to interact with the environment, such as cutting through obstacles or deflecting laser beams to solve puzzles. Recognizing these opportunities enhances both immersion and gameplay.

3.2 FORCE POWERS: USAGE AND STRATEGIES

The Force is what sets a Jedi apart, providing abilities that range from offensive attacks to defensive maneuvers. Each character's Force powers complement their combat style, offering a strategic layer to gameplay.

Offensive Force Powers

1. **Force Push**: This ability is invaluable for knocking back enemies, especially in tight spaces or when facing multiple foes. Use it strategically to create breathing room.
2. **Force Lightning** (Plo Koon): Deals area damage to surrounding enemies, ideal for crowd control.
3. **Force Sphere** (Darth Maul): A powerful projectile attack that deals significant damage to enemies in its path.

Defensive Force Powers

1. **Force Heal**: Essential for sustaining health during extended battles. Timing is crucial, as healing leaves you vulnerable for a moment.
2. **Force Block**: Reduces incoming damage and reflects blaster bolts, providing a defensive edge.

Utility Force Powers

1. **Force Jump**: Enhances jumping capabilities, allowing players to reach higher platforms or evade ground-based attacks.
2. **Force Sense**: Highlights hidden items or paths, encouraging exploration.

Strategies for Effective Force Usage

- **Energy Management**: Force powers consume energy, so use them sparingly and strategically. Collect Force energy orbs to replenish your reserves.
- **Combo Integration**: Combine Force powers with lightsaber attacks for maximum effectiveness. For example, use Force Push to stagger enemies before launching into a lightsaber combo.

3.3 COMBOS AND SPECIAL MOVES

Combos are the cornerstone of combat in *Jedi Power Battles*. They allow players to chain attacks for increased damage and style. Each character has unique combos that reflect their personality and fighting style.

Basic Combos

1. **Triple Slash**: A simple three-hit combo that's effective against standard enemies.
2. **Spin Attack**: Deals damage in a circular radius, perfect for clearing out groups.

Advanced Combos

1. **Juggle Combos**: Launch enemies into the air with an upward strike, then follow up with aerial attacks.
2. **Force-Enhanced Combos**: Incorporate Force powers into your attack sequence for devastating results. For example, use Force Pull to draw enemies closer before unleashing a combo.

Character-Specific Moves

- **Mace Windu's Power Slam**: A heavy attack that deals area damage.
- **Plo Koon's Lightning Strike**: Combines Force Lightning with a spinning lightsaber attack.

3.4 DEFENSIVE TACTICS AND DODGING

Defense is just as important as offense in *Jedi Power Battles*. Knowing how to dodge, block, and counterattack will keep you alive in the game's most challenging encounters.

Blocking and Deflecting

- **Blaster Deflection**: Timing your block to deflect blaster bolts back at enemies is not only effective but also satisfying.
- **Melee Blocks**: Blocking melee attacks reduces damage but requires precise timing.

Dodging

Dodging is essential for avoiding heavy attacks and environmental hazards. Each character's agility affects their dodging effectiveness, so choose your Jedi accordingly.

Environmental Awareness

Pay attention to your surroundings. Use pillars, walls, and other structures as cover to avoid incoming fire. Positioning can make all the difference in tough battles.

CHAPTER 4: LEVEL 1 - TRADE FEDERATION BATTLESHIP

4.1 WALKTHROUGH: CORRIDOR NAVIGATION AND DROID COMBAT

The Trade Federation Battleship is the first step on your journey, setting the tone for the challenges ahead. This level introduces players to core mechanics, combat strategies, and the galaxy's droid adversaries. Attention to detail and mastery of timing will ensure your success.

Navigating the Corridors

The battleship is a maze of narrow corridors and interconnected rooms. Stick to these tips to traverse it efficiently:

- **Follow the Objective Markers**: Use the visual markers to guide your path. These often point towards objectives or key areas.
- **Be Methodical**: The level is linear but has offshoot paths containing valuable items. Explore these cautiously but always return to the main route.
- **Watch for Ambushes**: Droids patrol the hallways in predictable patterns. Use corners and walls to your advantage, ambushing them before they spot you.

Combat with Battle Droids

The level is populated with basic battle droids perfect for practicing your combat skills. Here's how to handle them:

- **Close Combat**: Use quick lightsaber slashes to take down droids efficiently. Keep moving to avoid being surrounded.
- **Blaster Bolt Deflection**: Time your blocks to reflect enemy fire back at them. This is particularly useful against groups.
- **Force Powers**: Force Push can knock multiple droids off balance, giving you a brief respite to reposition or attack.

Key Areas to Note

- **Control Room**: Destroy the computer panels here to earn bonus points and disable certain enemy reinforcements.
- **Health Pickups**: Look for hidden alcoves containing health orbs, especially before combat-heavy sections.
- **Save Points**: Use these strategically to avoid losing progress.

4.2 BOSS STRATEGY: LOADER DROID

The Loader Droid is the level's first major challenge, combining brute strength with surprising agility. Understanding its attack patterns is crucial to defeating it.

Phase 1: Recognizing Attack Patterns

1. **Swipe Attacks**: The Loader Droid's arms swing in wide arcs. Dodge to the sides to avoid damage.
2. **Overhead Slam**: When it lifts both arms, prepare to roll away. The slam causes area damage and can stun you briefly.

3. **Charge Attack**: The droid occasionally charges forward. Sidestep or use a Force Jump to evade.

Phase 2: Counterattacking

- **Target Weak Points**: The droid's joints are vulnerable after an attack. Use this window to land heavy lightsaber combos.
- **Use the Environment**: Lead the droid into obstacles or confined areas, limiting its movement.
- **Force Powers**: Use Force Push to stagger the droid after it completes a charge, creating an opening for attacks.

Final Tips

- **Patience is Key**: Don't rush into attacks. Wait for openings to maximize damage while avoiding unnecessary risks.
- **Health Management**: Keep an eye on your health and grab orbs as needed. The Loader Droid hits hard, so staying topped off is crucial.

4.3 HIDDEN POWER-UPS AND POINTS GUIDE

The Trade Federation Battleship hides valuable power-ups and point bonuses for players willing to explore. These items not only enhance your abilities but also improve your score, unlocking bonuses at the end of the level.

Power-Up Locations

1. **First Corridor**: After defeating the initial group of droids, look to the left for a breakable crate containing a health orb.
2. **Control Room**: Destroy all the computer panels to reveal an energy boost.
3. **Conveyor Belt Area**: Jump to the upper platform to find a lightsaber power-up.
4. **Near the Loader Droid**: Before entering the boss room, search the right-hand corner for a Force energy refill.

Point Bonuses

Earn additional points by completing the following objectives:

- **Combo Mastery**: Execute long combo chains to receive a combo bonus.
- **Hidden Targets**: Destroy all crates, panels, and optional enemies for an environmental bonus.
- **Speed Bonus**: Complete the level under a certain time to earn a speed-run reward.

Pro Tips

- **Replay for Mastery**: You may need multiple attempts to collect all power-ups and achieve maximum points.
- **Track Collectibles**: Use the pause menu to check your progress on hidden items and objectives.
- **Use Force Sense**: This ability highlights nearby secrets, making exploration more rewarding.

4.4 AVOIDING CONVEYOR BELT HAZARDS

The conveyor belt section is one of the trickiest parts of the level, requiring precision and timing. Falling or being hit mid-air can result in instant failure, so approach with caution.

Navigating the Conveyor Belts

- **Jump Timing**: Double-jump across gaps to ensure safe landings. Watch for moving platforms and time your jumps carefully.
- **Avoiding Hazards**: The belts have laser traps and debris. Use short bursts of movement to avoid standing in one place too long.
- **Combat on the Belts**: Enemies will spawn on some conveyor belts. Knock them off with Force Push to clear the path.

Checkpoint Management

1. **Reaching Save Points**: Use save points strategically in this section to avoid replaying lengthy parts of the level.
2. **Health Conservation**: Collect health orbs between conveyor belts to ensure you're prepared for the next section.

Expert Tips for Mastery

- **Practice Makes Perfect**: The conveyor belts are a skill check. Replaying this section improves your timing and confidence.

- **Stay Centered**: Position yourself in the middle of platforms to reduce the risk of falling.
- **Focus on Movement**: Prioritize navigation over combat. It's better to avoid enemies than risk a fall.

By mastering the Trade Federation Battleship's intricacies, players will build a strong foundation for the challenges ahead. This level not only tests your reflexes but also introduces mechanics that will be crucial in later stages. Take your time, learn the patterns, and enjoy the satisfaction of conquering this iconic starting point in *Jedi Power Battles*.

CHAPTER 5: LEVEL 2 - SWAMPS OF NABOO

5.1 NAVIGATING THE SWAMP AND TREE CLIMB

The Swamps of Naboo present players with their first outdoor challenge in *Jedi Power Battles*. This level is as treacherous as it is beautiful, with murky waters, towering trees, and dangerous wildlife creating a rich yet hazardous environment. Mastering this level requires a blend of patience, precision, and strategic planning.

Understanding the Swamp's Layout

The swamp is divided into distinct sections, each with unique obstacles and enemies. The initial area is a maze of waterlogged paths, while the latter half shifts to elevated tree platforms and precarious jumps. Staying mindful of your surroundings is crucial to avoid getting ambushed by enemies or falling into environmental hazards.

Key Tips for Navigation

1. **Stick to the High Ground**: Where possible, take elevated routes to avoid enemy swarms and hidden traps.
2. **Watch for Hazards**: The swamp is littered with sinking platforms and venomous plants. Jump quickly off unstable surfaces to stay safe.
3. **Enemy Encounters**: Battle droids and swamp creatures will attack you frequently. Use quick lightsaber combos to dispatch them before they can surround you.
4. **Exploration**: Hidden power-ups and health pickups are scattered throughout the level. Explore side paths and climbable areas to find these valuable resources.

Climbing the Trees

The tree-climbing sections of this level test your platforming skills. Time your jumps carefully to avoid falling, and use Force Jump to reach higher branches. Remember to scan your surroundings for enemies before making a move, as many creatures hide among the foliage, ready to ambush unsuspecting players.

5.2 STAMPEDE AVOIDANCE TACTICS

Halfway through the level, you'll encounter one of the game's most iconic moments: the stampede. Massive creatures will charge through the swamp, creating a chaotic and deadly obstacle. Surviving this section requires quick reflexes and precise timing.

The Stampede Mechanics

The stampede begins suddenly, with a herd of wild animals barreling toward you. The narrow paths and waterlogged terrain make it difficult to dodge, so preparation is key.

Strategies for Survival

1. **Stick to the Sides**: Move to the edges of the path to minimize your chances of being trampled. Watch for safe spots where you can momentarily avoid the herd.
2. **Jumping Timing**: In areas where the path narrows, use double jumps to leap over incoming creatures. Avoid mid-air attacks during this section, as they can leave you vulnerable.

3. **Utilize Force Abilities**: Use Force Push to clear small creatures that obstruct your path and Force Jump to bypass particularly dangerous areas.
4. **Stay Calm**: Panicking can lead to mistimed jumps or unnecessary damage. Focus on timing your movements and maintaining a steady pace.

The stampede is a test of your reflexes and awareness, but with practice, you'll navigate this chaotic section unscathed.

5.3 GUNGAN ARTIFACT LOCATION

The Swamps of Naboo are home to the first of three Gungan Artifacts hidden throughout the game. Collecting these artifacts unlocks bonus content and enhances your overall score. Locating and retrieving the artifact in this level requires sharp observation and precise platforming.

Where to Find the Artifact

The artifact is located in the cavernous area of the swamp, just past the Y-shaped chasm. Look for a small, hidden platform near the bottom of the chasm that leads to the artifact's location. The platform is not immediately visible, so take your time exploring.

Steps to Collect the Artifact

1. **Reach the Y-Shaped Chasm**: Progress through the level until you reach this distinct landmark.
2. **Scan the Area**: Carefully examine the edges of the chasm for a hidden platform. You'll notice a faint glow marking the artifact's location.
3. **Force Jump Precision**: Use Force Jump to descend to the platform safely. Timing is critical, as missing the platform will result in falling into the abyss.
4. **Retrieve the Artifact**: Once on the platform, grab the artifact and prepare for a challenging climb back to the main path.

Tips for Success

- **Eliminate Nearby Enemies**: Clear out any creatures in the area before attempting to retrieve the artifact to avoid interruptions.
- **Save Your Progress**: If you're playing on an emulator or modern console, use save states to retry this tricky section if needed.

5.4 BOSS STRATEGY: GIANT WORM

The Giant Worm is the Swamps of Naboo's final challenge, serving as a formidable boss fight that tests your ability to adapt and strategize. This creature uses a combination of poison breath, tail swipes, and crushing attacks to overwhelm players.

Understanding the Giant Worm's Attacks

1. **Poison Breath**: The worm spews a cloud of poison that lingers in the area, causing damage over time. Keep moving to avoid prolonged exposure.
2. **Tail Swipe**: A quick, wide attack that can knock you off balance. Dodge to the side to avoid getting hit.
3. **Crushing Lunge**: The worm rears back before lunging forward, attempting to crush you. This attack has a brief wind-up, giving you time to react.

Strategies to Defeat the Giant Worm

1. **Focus on Mobility**: Constant movement is crucial to avoid the worm's attacks. Use your agility to stay out of its range and reposition yourself as needed.
2. **Attack During Vulnerable Moments**: The worm becomes vulnerable after it performs a tail swipe or poison breath attack. Use these moments to land heavy lightsaber combos or Force attacks.
3. **Use the Environment**: The swamp's terrain offers opportunities to gain the upper hand. Climb onto elevated platforms to avoid the worm's lunges and gain a better vantage point for attacks.
4. **Clear Kreetles**: Smaller creatures, known as Kreetles, will spawn during the fight to distract you. Take them out quickly to focus on the boss.

Phase Two: The Cave

After dealing significant damage, the worm retreats into a nearby cave for the second phase of the fight. Here, the terrain becomes more confined, and the worm gains new attack patterns.

Key Tactics for Phase Two

- **Stay Behind the Worm**: Position yourself behind the worm to avoid its frontal attacks. Use quick slashes to deal consistent damage.
- **Avoid the Tail Swipe**: Watch for the worm's tail movements and dodge when it winds up for a swipe.
- **Finish Strong**: Once the worm's health drops below 25%, it becomes more aggressive. Use all available Force powers and combos to end the fight quickly.

Defeating the Giant Worm is a satisfying accomplishment, showcasing your growth as a player. Celebrate your victory and prepare for the challenges ahead in the City of Theed.

CHAPTER 6: LEVEL 3 - CITY OF THEED

6.1 HANDMAIDEN RESCUE LOCATIONS

The City of Theed is one of the most iconic locations in *Star Wars: Episode I: Jedi Power Battles*, combining intense combat, platforming challenges, and rescue missions. A key objective in this level is to rescue seven handmaidens scattered across the city. Knowing their locations and how to safely reach them is crucial for success.

First Handmaiden

The first handmaiden is relatively easy to find. After progressing through the opening section of the level and defeating the initial wave of droids, you'll come to a courtyard. The handmaiden is located in the top right corner of this area. Dispatch the nearby droids quickly and approach her to complete the rescue.

Second Handmaiden

After navigating a series of narrow streets, you'll encounter a large staircase. Instead of ascending immediately, look for a narrow ledge on the left-hand side. Carefully jump onto this ledge and follow it around the building. The second handmaiden is hiding near a small alcove. Be cautious of enemy ambushes as you approach.

Third and Fourth Handmaidens

These handmaidens are located near a large fountain in the central plaza. As you enter the area, you'll notice droids patrolling both ground and elevated positions. Use ranged attacks to clear the enemies before rescuing the handmaidens. One is near the fountain itself, while the other is positioned on a balcony accessible via a series of jumps.

Fifth Handmaiden

The fifth handmaiden is found along the low road, hidden behind a set of crates near a destroyed speeder. If you chose the high road path earlier, you'll need to backtrack to access this location. Be prepared for a challenging encounter with destroyer droids guarding the area.

Sixth Handmaiden

After obtaining the AAT tank, use it to clear a path through enemy forces until you reach a walled courtyard. Exit the tank and proceed to the left side of the area, where you'll find the sixth handmaiden. Watch out for enemy reinforcements that may spawn as you approach.

Seventh Handmaiden

The final handmaiden is located just before the boss encounter. She is positioned near a series of bushes and trees in an open field. Clear the area of enemies before approaching to ensure a safe rescue. Completing this objective will reward you with bonus points and power-ups.

6.2 LOW ROAD VS. HIGH ROAD: WHICH PATH TO TAKE

The City of Theed offers two distinct paths the low road and the high road. Each path presents unique challenges and rewards, and choosing the right one depends on your playstyle and objectives.

Low Road

The low road is a ground-level path that emphasizes combat over platforming. This route is packed with enemies, including battle droids and destroyer droids, making it ideal for players who excel in direct combat. Additionally, the low road features more power-ups and health pickups, rewarding players who can handle the increased difficulty.

Key Features of the Low Road

1. **High Enemy Density**: Be prepared for waves of enemies that test your combat skills.
2. **Hidden Handmaiden**: The fifth handmaiden can only be accessed via the low road.
3. **Extra Points**: Defeating enemies and finding hidden pickups along this route can significantly boost your score.

High Road

The high road is a more platforming-intensive path that requires precise jumping and timing. It offers fewer enemies but introduces environmental hazards, such as collapsing platforms and rocket-firing droids. This path is better suited for players who prefer agility and exploration.

Key Features of the High Road

1. **Platforming Challenges**: Navigate narrow ledges and time your jumps carefully.
2. **Alternate Routes**: Discover hidden shortcuts that lead to power-ups and bonus points.
3. **Reduced Combat**: While there are fewer enemies, the ones you face are strategically positioned to maximize difficulty.

Recommendation

If you're looking to maximize your score and collect all handmaidens, the low road is the better choice. However, if you prefer a faster and less combat-intensive route, the high road offers a more streamlined experience.

6.3 USING THE AAT TANK EFFECTIVELY

The AAT (Armored Assault Tank) is a powerful tool that players can use to clear out enemies and obstacles in the City of Theed. Mastering its controls and understanding its capabilities will make your journey through this level much smoother.

Acquiring the AAT Tank

The tank becomes available midway through the level, shortly after rescuing the third and fourth handmaidens. Approach the vehicle and press the action button to board it. Once inside, you'll have access to its heavy cannon and durable armor.

Controls

1. **Movement**: The tank moves slower than your character but can navigate most terrain. Use the directional pad or joystick to steer.
2. **Cannon Fire**: Press the attack button to fire the tank's main cannon. This weapon is effective against both enemy droids and destructible objects.
3. **Shielding**: While the tank lacks a traditional shield, its armor can absorb significant damage, allowing you to engage enemies head-on.

Strategies for Effective Use

- **Clearing Obstacles**: Use the tank's cannon to destroy barriers and open new paths.

- **Enemy Engagement**: The tank excels at dealing with groups of droids. Position yourself at a distance to maximize the effectiveness of your cannon fire.
- **Exiting and Re-boarding**: In some areas, you may need to exit the tank to navigate tight spaces or interact with objects. Always return to the tank when possible to maintain its combat advantage.

Limitations

While the AAT is powerful, it's not invincible. Avoid over-relying on the tank, as certain enemies and environmental hazards can still pose a threat. Use it strategically to complement your Jedi's abilities.

6.4 BOSS STRATEGY: DROIDEKA DEFENSE DROID

The Droideka Defense Droid is a formidable boss that tests your combat and defensive skills. Known for its rapid blaster fire and impenetrable energy shield, this enemy requires a mix of strategy and precision to defeat.

Phase 1: Initial Encounter

The battle begins with the Droideka activating its shield and firing blaster bolts in rapid succession. Your first priority is to avoid damage while identifying openings for attack.

Key Strategies

1. **Deflecting Blaster Bolts**: Use your lightsaber to deflect the Droideka's shots back at it. This tactic deals damage and creates opportunities for counterattacks.
2. **Dodging**: Move constantly to avoid being overwhelmed by its rapid fire. Use rolls and sidesteps to evade incoming attacks.

Phase 2: Shield Down

Once the Droideka's shield is down, it becomes vulnerable to direct attacks. This phase is your chance to deal significant damage, but be cautious the Droideka will attempt to recharge its shield.

Key Strategies

1. **Close-Range Combos**: Move in quickly and unleash your most powerful combos. Characters with high damage output, such as Mace Windu, excel in this phase.
2. **Interrupting the Recharge**: Use Force abilities or ranged attacks to interrupt the Droideka's shield recharge process. Timing is critical to prevent it from regaining its defenses.

Phase 3: Final Assault

In the final phase, the Droideka becomes more aggressive, using melee attacks and deploying mines. This phase demands heightened awareness and adaptability.

Key Strategies

1. **Keep Your Distance**: Maintain a safe distance to avoid melee attacks and focus on ranged damage.
2. **Destroy Mines**: Clear any mines the Droideka deploys to prevent unnecessary damage.
3. **Finish Strong**: Time your attacks carefully to land the final blow before the Droideka can counter.

Rewards

Defeating the Droideka Defense Droid rewards you with bonus points, power-ups, and progression to the next level. It's a challenging fight, but mastering its mechanics will leave you feeling accomplished and ready for the challenges ahead.

The City of Theed is a standout level in *Jedi Power Battles*, combining intricate level design with engaging combat and strategic objectives. By mastering the handmaiden rescues, choosing the optimal path, utilizing the AAT tank, and defeating the Droideka Defense Droid, you'll conquer this iconic Star Wars location with style and efficiency.

CHAPTER 7: LEVEL 5 - TATOOINE

7.1 PROTECTING ANAKIN AND RETRIEVING THE HYPERDRIVE

Tatooine, a desolate desert planet, presents a stark contrast to the lush swamps of Naboo or the grandeur of Theed. In this level, your primary objectives are to protect young Anakin Skywalker and retrieve the stolen hyperdrive needed to escape the planet. Success requires a balance of combat prowess, environmental awareness, and strategic planning.

Escort Mission Mechanics

The level begins with a classic escort scenario. Anakin, while skilled with machinery, is defenseless against the hostile forces on Tatooine. As you progress, enemies will relentlessly target him. It is your duty to ensure his safety.

- **Stay Close to Anakin**: Keep an eye on his position at all times. Straying too far from him could lead to him being overwhelmed by enemies.
- **Prioritize Threats**: Focus on enemies closest to Anakin. Battle droids and Tusken Raiders often emerge in waves, targeting him directly.
- **Use Force Abilities Strategically**: Force Push can be used to knock back groups of enemies, buying Anakin time to move.

Finding the Hyperdrive

As you navigate the dunes, you'll encounter a series of small settlements and caves. These areas are riddled with enemies and traps but also contain clues about the hyperdrive's location.

- **Search Thoroughly**: Investigate every dwelling and crate for useful items and information about the hyperdrive's whereabouts.
- **Beware of Ambushes**: Probe droids and Tusken snipers often lie in wait. Use cover and take them out quickly.
- **Follow the Map**: The level's map highlights key locations to explore, minimizing time spent wandering.

7.2 SURVIVING SANDSTORMS AND PROBE DROIDS

Tatooine's unforgiving environment adds another layer of difficulty to this level. Sandstorms reduce visibility and hinder movement, while probe droids patrol the area, ready to attack at a moment's notice.

Navigating Sandstorms

Sandstorms are a recurring hazard throughout the level. They obscure your vision and can disorient you, making it easy to miss objectives or fall into enemy ambushes.

- **Use Landmarks**: Look for large rocks, moisture vaporators, and other landmarks to orient yourself during sandstorms.
- **Move Slowly**: Rushing through the storm can lead to mistakes. Take your time to avoid falling into enemy traps.

- **Listen for Audio Cues**: The sound of enemies or Anakin's calls for help can guide you through the blinding sands.

Dealing with Probe Droids

Probe droids are mobile and can detect you from a distance, launching laser attacks that are difficult to dodge.

- **Take the High Ground**: Climb onto ledges and rooftops to spot probe droids before they detect you.
- **Aim for Weak Spots**: Probe droids are vulnerable to precise attacks. Use ranged Force abilities or deflect their shots back at them.
- **Eliminate Quickly**: The longer you leave probe droids active, the more likely they are to alert other enemies.

7.3 GUNGAN ARTIFACT COLLECTION

Hidden throughout the level are rare Gungan artifacts. Collecting these not only adds to your overall score but also unlocks bonuses and concept art in the game's extras menu.

Locating Artifacts

There are three Gungan artifacts hidden across Tatooine. Each requires exploration and careful observation to locate.

1. **The Desert Dwelling**: The first artifact is in an abandoned house near the yellow sand slope. Enter the dwelling and search thoroughly. Be prepared to fight off a small group of Tusken Raiders.
2. **The Canyon's Hidden Path**: The second artifact is located in a canyon. Look for a narrow path leading to a secluded area. Jump across gaps and avoid falling rocks to reach the artifact.
3. **The Sarlaac's Lair**: The final artifact is dangerously close to a Sarlaac pit. Use Force Jump to navigate the terrain safely. Watch out for Tusken ambushes and retrieve the artifact quickly.

Tips for Artifact Collection

- **Explore Off the Main Path**: Artifacts are often hidden in areas not required to complete the level.
- **Be Prepared for Combat**: Enemies frequently guard artifact locations. Clear them out before attempting to collect the artifact.

- **Use the Map**: Pay attention to map markers indicating areas of interest. These often lead to artifact locations.

7.4 BOSS STRATEGY: DARTH MAUL

The climax of the Tatooine level pits you against Darth Maul, one of the most formidable adversaries in the game. This duel tests your mastery of combat mechanics and requires both strategy and skill.

Phase 1: Initial Engagement

Darth Maul begins the fight with aggressive lightsaber attacks and Force abilities. His double-bladed lightsaber allows him to attack from multiple angles, making him a challenging opponent.

- **Block and Dodge**: Use your block ability to deflect his strikes and dodge-roll to avoid his wide-range attacks.
- **Maintain Distance**: Darth Maul excels in close combat. Use Force Push or ranged attacks to create space.
- **Counterattack**: Wait for openings after his heavy attacks to land quick combos.

Phase 2: Strategic Terrain Use

As the fight progresses, the battlefield shifts. Platforms crumble, and environmental hazards come into play.

- **Watch Your Footing**: Avoid falling off ledges or into environmental traps.
- **Use Height Advantages**: Jump to higher platforms to gain a tactical edge over Maul.
- **Exploit Power-Ups**: Look for health or Force power-ups scattered across the arena.

Phase 3: Final Showdown

In the final phase, Darth Maul becomes even more aggressive, combining lightsaber strikes with Force Choke and other abilities.

- **Keep Moving**: Staying in one place makes you an easy target for his Force abilities.
- **Interrupt His Combos**: Use Force abilities like Push or Pull to disrupt his attacks.
- **Finish with Style**: Time your final blows carefully to end the battle in cinematic fashion.

Mastering the Tatooine level requires a combination of combat skills, environmental awareness, and strategic thinking. Protecting Anakin, surviving the harsh environment, and facing Darth Maul will push you to your limits, but with perseverance, you'll emerge victorious.

CHAPTER 8: BONUS LEVELS AND CHALLENGES

8.1 LEVEL 11: DROIDEKAS

Level 11, also known as "Droidekas," offers a thrilling twist to the standard gameplay of *Jedi Power Battles*. In this level, players take on the role of a destroyer droid, rolling and blasting their way through waves of enemies. This unique perspective allows players to explore a non-Jedi approach to combat while mastering the destroyer droid's distinct abilities.

Objectives

1. Eliminate all 18 pilot droids scattered across the level.
2. Defeat two Jedi adversaries in the final showdown.

Gameplay Tips

- **Rolling Mechanic**: Use the rolling ability to quickly traverse the map and avoid enemy fire. This maneuver also helps close the gap between enemies and yourself.

- **Wide-Range Blaster Fire**: The destroyer droid's primary attack covers a large area, making it ideal for dealing with groups of enemies. Use it strategically to maximize damage.
- **Blocking**: Take advantage of the droid's energy shield to deflect incoming attacks. Timing your blocks effectively can save you from taking unnecessary damage.

Key Challenges

- **Enemy Positioning**: Many pilot droids are positioned in elevated areas or behind cover, requiring precise aim and strategy to eliminate them.
- **Jedi Opponents**: The final encounter pits you against two Jedi. Use hit-and-run tactics to avoid their lightsaber attacks while landing shots from a safe distance.

Completing this level successfully unlocks a sense of empowerment as players experience the game from a completely different angle, showcasing the versatility of the gameplay.

8.2 LEVEL 12: KAADU RACE

The "Kaadu Race" is a fast-paced level that challenges players to channel their inner podracer. This level is a departure from traditional combat and focuses on speed, precision, and timing as players compete in a high-stakes race.

Objectives

1. Win the race by reaching the finish line before your opponent.
2. Collect power-ups along the way to boost your performance.

Gameplay Tips

- **Alternate Button Pressing**: To achieve maximum speed, alternate between the Square and Circle buttons rapidly. Consistent button pressing ensures you maintain momentum.
- **Obstacle Avoidance**: The racecourse is littered with obstacles, such as rocks and low-hanging branches. Anticipate these hazards and maneuver accordingly.

- **Power-Up Collection**: Scattered throughout the course are speed boosts and health packs. Prioritize collecting these to maintain an edge over your opponent.

Key Challenges

- **Tight Corners**: Many sections of the track require sharp turns. Use the Kaadu's agility to navigate these effectively without losing speed.
- **Dynamic Opponent AI**: Your competitor adapts to your movements, making it crucial to stay unpredictable and maintain a lead.

Winning the Kaadu Race rewards players with a sense of accomplishment and unlocks additional content, further enriching the game's replay value.

8.3 LEVEL 13: GUNGAN ROUNDUP

"Gungan Roundup" combines humor and skill as players guide Jar Jar Binks and other Gungans to safety. This level emphasizes crowd control and strategic positioning to achieve the objectives.

Objectives

1. Locate all three Gungan Artifacts hidden throughout the level.
2. Herd Jar Jar Binks toward the goal area without losing him to enemy attacks.
3. Score three goals in the "Gungan Roundup" minigame to unlock the Concept Art Gallery.

Gameplay Tips

- **Artifact Locations**: Carefully explore the map to uncover hidden artifacts. Use the Force Sense ability if available to highlight these locations.
- **Crowd Control**: Enemies will try to disrupt your progress by targeting Jar Jar. Prioritize eliminating these threats quickly.
- **Strategic Herding**: Position yourself to guide Jar Jar along the safest paths. Use Force Push to clear obstacles or redirect him if necessary.

Key Challenges

- **Enemy Waves**: As you progress, the number of enemies increases. Stay vigilant and use area-of-effect attacks to manage the crowd.
- **Jar Jar's AI**: His erratic movements can make herding difficult. Patience is key to ensuring he reaches the goal safely.

Completing "Gungan Roundup" is as rewarding as it is entertaining, offering a lighter, comedic break from the game's intense action.

8.4 LEVEL 14: SURVIVAL CHALLENGE

The "Survival Challenge" is the ultimate test of endurance and skill in *Jedi Power Battles*. Players must defeat waves of enemies from every type encountered throughout the game, culminating in the ultimate saber mode where every hit is a one-hit kill.

Objectives

1. Defeat 10 enemies of each type to progress through the waves.

2. Survive long enough to unlock the Ultimate Saber Mode.

Gameplay Tips

- **Prioritize Targets**: Some enemies are more dangerous than others. Focus on eliminating high-priority threats, such as destroyer droids, first.
- **Use the Environment**: Position yourself near chokepoints or obstacles to funnel enemies and control the battlefield.
- **Health Management**: Conserve health by dodging attacks and collecting health pickups whenever possible.

Key Challenges

- **Enemy Variety**: Each wave introduces new enemy types, requiring players to adapt their strategies on the fly.
- **Stamina**: The length of this level tests your endurance. Pace yourself and avoid unnecessary risks.
- **Final Waves**: The last few waves are the most intense, featuring multiple high-level enemies simultaneously.

Surviving the "Survival Challenge" grants players a sense of mastery over the game's mechanics and showcases their progress as a true Jedi warrior.

Chapter 8 delivers a mix of fun, strategy, and challenges, making these bonus levels a highlight of *Jedi Power Battles*. Whether you're racing Kaadu, herding Gungans, or battling endless waves of enemies, each level offers a unique experience that enriches the overall gameplay.

CHAPTER 9: ADVANCED TIPS AND SECRETS

9.1 MAXIMIZING POINTS AND BONUSES

In *Star Wars: Episode I: Jedi Power Battles*, achieving high scores and unlocking bonuses is not only rewarding but also essential for mastering the game. The key lies in understanding the scoring system and leveraging every opportunity to earn points.

Understanding the Scoring System

Each action you perform contributes to your overall score. Points are awarded for defeating enemies, collecting power-ups, and completing objectives. Here's a breakdown:

- **Defeating Enemies**: Higher points are awarded for chaining combos and using advanced attacks.
- **Collectibles**: Picking up health, Force power-ups, and extra lives adds to your score.

- **Completion Bonuses**: Achieving specific goals within levels, such as time-based challenges or not taking damage, rewards bonus points.

Combos and Multipliers

Executing combos is one of the fastest ways to accumulate points. Stringing together multiple attacks without interruption activates a multiplier, significantly boosting your score.

Tips for Effective Combos:

1. **Mix Up Attacks**: Alternate between light and heavy attacks to keep combos flowing.
2. **Incorporate Force Powers**: Using abilities like Force Push or Force Pull mid-combo can extend the chain.
3. **Avoid Damage**: Getting hit resets your combo multiplier, so focus on dodging and blocking.

Time-Based Challenges

Many levels offer time-based objectives that reward bonus points. Completing sections quickly without sacrificing precision is key.

Pro Tip: Use characters like Plo Koon or Adi Gallia, whose agility makes them well-suited for speed runs.

9.2 UNLOCKING CONCEPT ART AND EXTRAS

The game features a variety of unlockable extras, including concept art, alternate costumes, and bonus levels. These rewards add depth to the game and provide additional motivation for completionists.

Concept Art

Unlocking concept art requires achieving specific goals in each level. This might include:

- **Perfect Scores**: Earning all available points in a level.
- **Hidden Objectives**: Completing secret tasks, such as finding all Gungan artifacts or rescuing all handmaidens.

Tips for Unlocking Concept Art:

1. **Replay Levels**: Revisiting earlier levels with improved skills can help you achieve perfect scores.

2. **Explore Thoroughly**: Check every nook and cranny for hidden items and objectives.
3. **Use Unlockable Characters**: Characters like Darth Maul offer unique abilities that can simplify certain challenges.

Alternate Costumes

Some characters have alternate costumes that are unlocked by completing the game under specific conditions. For example, finishing the game as Queen Amidala might unlock a royal gown skin.

Unlocking Tips:

- **Focus on Specific Characters**: Dedicate runs to mastering one character at a time.
- **Co-op Mode**: Partnering with a friend can make challenging objectives easier to accomplish.

Bonus Levels

Unlocking bonus levels like "Kaadu Race" or "Gungan Roundup" requires collecting specific artifacts or achieving high scores in previous stages.

Pro Tip: Completing the Survival Challenge in record time unlocks additional game modes, increasing replayability.

9.3 EXPLORING HIDDEN ROUTES AND POWER-UPS

Hidden routes and power-ups are scattered throughout the game, rewarding players who take the time to explore. These secrets often provide significant advantages, such as extra lives, health boosts, or bonus points.

Identifying Hidden Routes

Hidden paths are often marked by subtle visual cues, such as cracks in walls, unusual textures, or out-of-place objects.

Notable Hidden Routes:

1. **Theed Palace**: In the main hall, destroying specific windows reveals a hidden passage.
2. **Swamps of Naboo**: Look for mushrooms that form a natural bridge to an alternate route.

3. **Trade Federation Battleship**: Jumping onto conveyor belts at the right time leads to secret areas.

Power-Up Locations

Power-ups are often placed in hard-to-reach areas, rewarding skilled platforming and exploration.

Key Power-Ups:

- **Force Energy Boosts**: Found in corners of larger rooms or behind destructible objects.
- **Extra Lives**: Typically hidden in elevated areas requiring Force Jump to access.
- **Saber Enhancements**: Temporarily increase lightsaber damage and range.

Strategies for Exploration

1. **Take Your Time**: Rushing through levels often means missing key secrets.
2. **Use Force Abilities**: Powers like Force Jump and Force Sense reveal hidden paths and items.
3. **Replay Levels**: Many secrets are easier to find once you're familiar with the level design.

9.4 CO-OP MULTIPLAYER STRATEGIES

Co-op mode is one of the most enjoyable aspects of *Jedi Power Battles*. Teaming up with a friend not only enhances the experience but also opens up new tactical possibilities.

Teamwork and Coordination

Effective communication is the cornerstone of successful co-op gameplay. Assign roles based on each player's chosen character:

- **Tank and Damage Dealer**: One player focuses on absorbing damage (e.g., Mace Windu), while the other deals consistent damage (e.g., Plo Koon).
- **Crowd Control and Support**: Characters like Adi Gallia excel at crowd control, while others focus on dealing with stronger enemies.

Shared Resources

Health and power-ups are limited in co-op mode, so sharing is crucial:

- **Prioritize Health**: Allocate health pickups to the player with the lowest health or most critical role.
- **Manage Force Energy**: Coordinate Force power usage to ensure neither player runs out at a critical moment.

Combo Synergy

Combining attacks with a partner can lead to devastating results. For example:

- **Force Push and Aerial Attacks**: One player uses Force Push to stagger enemies, allowing the other to follow up with aerial combos.
- **Group Control**: Use area-of-effect abilities to manage groups of enemies while your partner focuses on single-target damage.

Advanced Tactics

1. **Divide and Conquer**: Split up to cover more ground and complete objectives faster, but regroup during tougher encounters.
2. **Choke Points**: Lure enemies into narrow spaces where both players can attack simultaneously.

3. **Boss Strategies**: Coordinate attack patterns to exploit boss weaknesses. For example, while one player distracts the boss, the other targets its vulnerabilities.

Pro Tip: Experiment with different character combinations to discover synergies that suit your playstyle.

By mastering these advanced tips and secrets, you'll not only enhance your gameplay experience but also unlock the full potential of *Star Wars: Episode I: Jedi Power Battles*. Whether you're hunting for hidden power-ups, achieving perfect scores, or dominating in co-op mode, these strategies will ensure your journey through the galaxy is both rewarding and unforgettable.

CHAPTER 10: FINAL BOSS AND ENDGAME STRATEGIES

10.1 LEVEL 10 WALKTHROUGH: THE FINAL BATTLE

The final level of *Star Wars: Episode I: Jedi Power Battles* is an epic conclusion that tests every skill you've honed throughout the game. Set on the perilous Energy Bridge within the depths of Naboo's plasma refinery, this level is a gauntlet of intense combat, environmental hazards, and the ultimate showdown with Darth Maul.

Preparing for the Final Battle

Before diving into Level 10, make sure your character's health and Force energy are as full as possible. Collect all power-ups in the previous levels and take note of the save point locations they're invaluable for retries.

Navigating the Initial Corridors

The opening segment begins with a series of tight corridors filled with droids and plasma hazards.

1. **Combat Awareness**: Be ready for ambushes from both sides. Reflect blaster bolts and clear droids methodically.
2. **Environmental Hazards**: Watch for plasma leaks on the floor. Jump over these hazards or time your movement to avoid taking damage.
3. **Hidden Power-Ups**: Some corners hide extra health and Force energy. Look for small alcoves as you progress.

Entering the Energy Bridge Arena

As you make your way to the main arena, you'll face a few advanced droid enemies, including grapple and rifle droids. Use ranged Force attacks to deal with groups efficiently.

10.2 BOSS STRATEGY: DEFEATING DARTH MAUL

Darth Maul is a multi-phase boss encounter designed to push your combat skills to the limit. His combination of dual-bladed lightsaber attacks and Force abilities makes him a formidable opponent. Each phase introduces new challenges, requiring adaptability and precision.

Phase One: Close-Quarters Combat

1. **Dual-Bladed Assaults**: Maul's attacks are fast and wide-ranging. Use the block button to deflect his initial strikes and look for openings to counter.
2. **Combo Avoidance**: Dodge his spinning saber combo by rolling sideways. Timing is crucial here a mistimed roll can lead to devastating damage.
3. **Force Push Vulnerability**: During his recovery from an attack, use Force Push to stagger him and follow up with quick combos.

Phase Two: Energy Bridge Showdown

Once you've depleted his first health bar, the battle transitions to the precarious Energy Bridge.

1. **Bridge Mechanics**: The bridge periodically emits pulses of energy that can knock you off. Keep an eye on the pulse patterns and move accordingly.
2. **Droid Interference**: Maul summons droids during this phase. Take them out quickly to avoid distractions.
3. **Counterattacks**: Maul uses a charging attack here. Dodge sideways and retaliate immediately.

Final Phase: Catwalk Duel

The battle moves to a series of narrow catwalks, upping the ante with limited movement space.

1. **Stay Centered**: Avoid fighting too close to the edges to prevent accidental falls.
2. **Force Lightning**: Maul frequently uses Force Lightning in this phase. Use Force Block to mitigate damage and counter with long-range attacks.
3. **Finishing Blow**: When his health is critically low, Maul becomes more aggressive. Stay defensive, wait for an opening, and deliver the final strike.

10.3 ENERGY BRIDGE AND CATWALK NAVIGATION

The Energy Bridge and subsequent catwalks are as much a test of platforming as they are combat. Precision, timing, and awareness are vital for survival.

Energy Bridge Navigation

1. **Timing Your Movement**: The bridge's energy pulses are predictable. Watch the timing and move during the safe intervals.
2. **Mid-Bridge Battles**: Enemies will spawn on the bridge. Use quick combos to dispatch them before the energy pulses return.
3. **Force Jumping**: Use Force Jump to traverse gaps and avoid energy surges when necessary.

Catwalk Challenges

1. **Narrow Paths**: The catwalks are narrow, with little room for error. Use careful positioning to avoid falling.

2. **Enemy Placement**: Enemies often appear on the catwalks to knock you off. Use ranged Force powers to eliminate them from a safe distance.
3. **Power-Up Management**: Hidden along the catwalks are critical health and Force power-ups. Look for subtle cues, such as faint glows, to locate these items.

10.4 LASER MAZE AND ULTIMATE VICTORY

The Laser Maze represents the final environmental obstacle before your ultimate confrontation with Darth Maul. Patience and precision are critical to overcoming this section.

Navigating the Laser Maze

1. **Observing Patterns**: The lasers move in specific patterns. Study their sequence before attempting to move forward.
2. **Safe Zones**: Identify safe zones between laser grids where you can pause and reassess your timing.

3. **Force-Assisted Movement**: Use Force Dash or Force Jump to quickly bypass particularly tricky sections.

Final Combat with Maul

After clearing the maze, you'll face Darth Maul one final time. The stakes are higher, but the strategies remain similar:

1. **Advanced Saber Techniques**: Use everything you've learned about lightsaber combat to keep the upper hand.
2. **Force Management**: Conserve your Force energy for critical moments, such as dodging his most powerful attacks.
3. **Endgame Finishers**: When Maul is near defeat, use your strongest combos to deliver the final blow and secure victory.

Celebration and Rewards

Upon defeating Darth Maul, you'll be treated to a cinematic ending and unlock bonus content, such as alternate costumes or concept art. Your journey through *Jedi Power Battles* culminates in a sense of accomplishment and mastery.

Chapter 10 serves as the ultimate test of your skills in *Star Wars: Episode I: Jedi Power Battles*. By applying the strategies outlined here, you'll be well-equipped to conquer the game's final challenges and emerge victorious in the galaxy far, far away.

www.ingramcontent.com/pod-product-compliance
Lightning Source LLC
Chambersburg PA
CBHW070203230526
45471CB00002B/793